Countries of the World

Thailand

by Kristin Thoennes

Consultant:
Soontareya Tandraprapan
Information Officer
Royal Thai Embassy

D1404096

Bridgestone Books
an imprint of Capstone Press
Mankato, Minnesota

Bridgestone Books are published by Capstone Press
818 North Willow Street, Mankato, Minnesota 56001
http://www.capstone-press.com

Library of Congress Cataloging-in-Publication Data
Thoennes, Kristin.
    Thailand/by Kristin Thoennes.
    p. cm.—(Countries of the world)
    Summary: Discusses the landscape, culture, food, animals, and sports of Thailand.
    Includes bibliographical references and index.
    ISBN 0-7368-0157-X
    1. Thailand—Juvenile literature. [1. Thailand.] I. Title. II. Series.
    DS563.5.T46   1999
    959.3—dc21
                                                                        98-42292
                                                                            CIP
                                                                             AC

Editorial Credits
Blanche R. Bolland, editor; Timothy Halldin, cover designer; Linda Clavel and Timothy Halldin,
    illustrators; Kimberly Danger and Sheri Gosewisch, photo researchers

Photo Credits
Betty Crowell, 16, 20
Jerry Ruff, 5 (bottom)
John Elk III, 8, 18
Maxine Cass, 6
PhotoBank, Inc./Michele Burgess, 12
Photri-Microstock, 10, 14
StockHaus Limited, 5 (top)
Uniphoto, cover

Table of Contents

Fast Facts

Name: Kingdom of Thailand
Capital: Bangkok
Population: More than 60 million
Languages: Thai, Chinese, Malay
Religion: Mostly Buddhist

Size: 198,115 square miles (513,118 square kilometers) *Thailand is about the size of the U.S. states of Arizona and Utah combined.*
Crops: Rice, corn, sugarcane

Maps

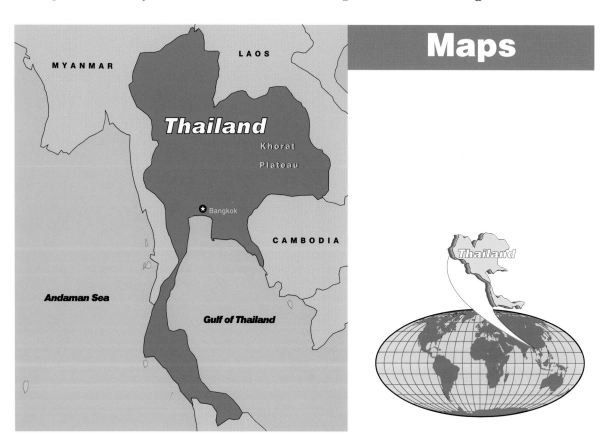

Flag

Thailand's flag has five horizontal stripes. The wide blue stripe in the center stands for the king and queen. Two white stripes are on either side of the blue stripe. The white stripes represent religion and purity. Two red outer stripes stand for Thailand.

Currency

The Thai unit of currency is the baht. One hundred satang equal 1 baht.

In the late 1990s, about 42 baht equaled 1 U.S. dollar. About 27 baht equaled 1 Canadian dollar.

The Land

Thailand lies in southeastern Asia. The Khorat Plateau in northeastern Thailand covers one-third of the country. Foothills of the Himalaya mountain range rise in the northwest. Forests grow on these high hills.

The central region of Thailand consists of flat plains. Rivers flow through the plains. Many of the rivers are canals made by people. Thais call these canals "klong." Rice grows in the wet fields of the central plains.

A long, narrow area of land stretches south along the Gulf of Thailand. Thick rain forests cover this mountainous region. Many rubber and coconut trees grow there. Islands lie off the coast.

Thailand has three seasons. From March to May, the weather is hot and dry. The rainy season lasts from June through October. Dry, cooler weather comes in November.

Thick forests grow on the foothills of the northwest.

Life at Home

Rivers are an important part of life in Thailand. People travel on rivers. Thais who live in the countryside bathe and play in rivers. People also carry river water to their crops.

Thais build wooden houses near rivers. The front door usually faces the river. Most houses sit high above the ground on stilts. The poles keep the houses dry if the rivers flood.

Less than 25 percent of Thais live in cities. Bangkok is the largest city. Many klong flow through Bangkok. Some people live in floating houses on klong. Others live above stores or factories. These homes are called shop houses.

Thailand's weather is hot most of the year. Thais find ways to stay cool. They cook outside to keep the heat out of their homes. Businesses open early in the morning when it is cool. Many people carry washcloths to wipe their faces.

Many Thai houses sit on stilts beside rivers.

Going to School

Children in Thailand attend school from ages 7 to 14. Most Thai schools require students to wear uniforms.

Grade-school students study math, science, and the Thai language. They also learn about history, geography, and religion. Thai children take music lessons. Children also learn traditional dances.

Most high schools are private. Parents pay money for their children to attend these schools. Students can choose from many courses. They can study math, history, or geography. They also can learn boxing or painting.

High school boys spend one month in special training. They learn about serving in the military. The boys wear uniforms like soldiers in the army wear.

Most Thai students wear uniforms.

Thai Food

Thais eat rice at most meals. People in the south like fluffy rice. People in the north prefer sticky rice. Thais eat rice with their fingers. Rice goes well with other common Thai foods.

People in Thailand like spicy foods. They add a spicy sauce to almost every dish. Nam pla prik (NAHM PLAH PRIG) is a popular pepper sauce. People in the south enjoy curry. This combination of spices comes from India.

Many meals include Thai salad. This mixture of fresh vegetables and fruits often includes meat or seafood. Cooks carefully arrange the salad and top it with peanuts.

Thais eat many fresh fruits. Bananas, mangoes, and pineapples grow in Thailand. Some fruits that grow in Thailand's hot climate have a strong flavor. Thais often buy and sell fruit from boats on klong. These boats are floating markets.

Thais often sell fruit from floating markets.

Animals

The most famous animal from Thailand is the Siamese cat. Thailand was once called Siam. Most people in Thailand do not have Siamese cats because cats eat lizards. People want lizards around because they eat mosquitos. Mosquito bites can make people sick.

Thai people use elephants and water buffalo to help them work. Thais train elephants to move heavy logs. Water buffalo pull plows or crush grain.

Thailand's rain forests are home to many animals. Tigers, leopards, and monkeys live there. Wild elephants roam the area. Cobras, vipers, and pythons are the deadliest snakes in Thailand.

Insects grow very large in the rain forests. Some moths have a wingspan of 1 foot (30 centimeters). Hundreds of different butterflies fly through Thailand's rain forests.

Water buffalo often work in Thailand's rice fields.

Clothing

Most Thais wear clothes like North Americans wear. Some people in villages wear clothes like Thais wore long ago. Thais often make this traditional clothing from colorful silk. Silkworms in Thailand produce the raw material for this shiny cloth.

Thais embroider colorful patterns on traditional clothing. Children learn this type of sewing at an early age.

People dress to keep cool in Thailand's hot weather. Women wear blouses and sarongs (sah-RAWNGS). Sarongs are long, narrow skirts that wrap around the waist. Thai men wear pants and shirts in public. But men sometimes dress in sarongs at home.

Thai clothing also keeps the head and feet cool. Many Thais wear straw hats to block the sun. People wear sandals called thongs.

Traditional clothing has embroidered patterns.

Sports and Games

Thai boxing is a popular sport in Thailand. Barefoot boxers kick or punch one another. Music often plays during the match. The boxers bounce to the beat of the music.

Many Thais play takraw (tak-RAW). This game is similar to both volleyball and soccer. Players try to keep the ball in the air. They cannot use their hands to hit the ball. They use their heads and feet to pass the ball over a net.

Kite fighting is popular in Thailand. Players use their kite to knock down other kites. The fight lasts until only one kite is in the air. In the spring, thousands of Thais watch kite fights near the Grand Palace in Bangkok.

The old sport of boat racing remains popular today. Teams consist of about 10 rowers. The teams race as part of celebrations at the end of the rainy season.

Takraw is a combination of volleyball and soccer.

Holidays

People celebrate the New Year twice in Thailand. Thais celebrate New Year's Day on January 1 like North Americans do. Thais cook eggs in soy sauce for New Year's. These eggs stand for a good life in the new year.

Songkran (sawng-KRAHN) is the other New Year holiday. Songkran lasts three days in April. Thais use water to clean buildings then. They also throw water at one another. The water cleans buildings and people for the new year.

Loy Krathong (LOY krah-TONG) comes at the end of the rainy season. People float tiny boats with burning candles on the rivers. Some Thais believe the boats will bring them good luck. Others celebrate Loy Krathong to thank the river for all it gives them.

The queen's and king's birthdays also are holidays in Thailand. Thais celebrate with parades.

Thais celebrate the king's birthday with boat parades.

Hands On: Play Fish

Thousands of different fish live in the seas off Thailand. Thais often buy fish at floating markets. Children in Thailand play the game of Fish. You can learn to play Fish, too.

What You Need
Six or more players   Blindfold

What You Do
1. Choose someone to be the fish. Tie a blindfold around the eyes of that person. Spin the fish around three times.
2. Have the other players form a circle around the fish.
3. Ask the fish if it is dead or alive. The other players can move around if the fish is dead. They must stay where they are if the fish is alive.
4. The fish should then try to catch someone. When the fish catches a player, ask it to name that person. If the guess is right, that person becomes the fish.
5. If the guess is wrong, repeat steps 3 and 4.

Learn to Speak Thai

father	por	(POR)
hello	sa wat dee	(SA WAT DEE)
mother	mair	(MAYR)
please	ga run ar	(GA RUN AR)
sorry	kor toet	(KOR TOHT)
thank you	korp kun	(KORP KUHN)
yes (females)	ka	(KAH)
yes (males)	krap	(KRAP)

Words to Know

canal (kuh-NAL)—a river made by people
curry (KUH-ree)—a powdered spice from India
embroider (em-BROI-dur)—to sew a pattern or picture onto cloth
plateau (pla-TOH)—an area of high, flat land
sarong (suh-RONG)—a piece of cloth wrapped around the waist
stilt (STILT)—a pole to hold something or someone above ground; many Thai homes near rivers are built on stilts.

Read More

Brittan, Dolly. *The People of Thailand.* Celebrating the Peoples and Civilizations of Southeast Asia. New York: PowerKid's Press, 1997.

Whyte, Harlinah. *Thailand.* Festivals of the World. Milwaukee: Gareth Stevens Publishing, 1998.

Useful Addresses and Internet Sites

Royal Thai Embassy
1024 Wisconsin Avenue NW
Washington, DC 20007

Royal Thai Embassy
180 Island Park Drive
Ottawa, ON K1P 6A9
Canada

ABC Country Book of Thailand
http://www.theodora.com/wfb/thailand_geography.html

Welcome to Thailand
http://www.asiatour.com/thailand/content1.htm

Index